Dance in the Dark

POETRY IN THE DEAD OF NIGHT

SHIRLEY SIATON

DANCE IN THE DARK:
Poetry in the dead of night

Copyright © 2023 Shirley Siaton-Parabia

ALL RIGHTS RESERVED.
No part of this book may be reproduced or used in any manner without the prior written permission of the copyright owner, except for the use of brief quotations in a book review. To request permission, contact the publisher at books@inkysword.com.

ISBN 978-6-21-837487-4 (pbk)

Published by Shirley S. Parabia
Illustrations by Rein Geronimo

First Edition, June 2023

Inky Sword Book Publishing
Barangay Quezon
Arevalo, Iloilo City 5000
Republic of the Philippines
inkysword.com

To Pagit
Yes, I still cause trouble wherever I go

SHIRLEY SIATON

CONTENTS

Acknowledgments   1

Introduction   3

The Dance   5

Part One: Emergence   9

Distance	13
Despair	15
Dark	17
Disruption	19
Deception	21
Discord	23
Debt	25
Delusion	27
Danger	29
Deprivation	31
Divination	33
Death	35

Part Two: Odyssey   37

Damnation   41
Dribble   43
Demolition   45
Dreams   47
Disease   49
Defiance   51
Duplication   53
Difference   55
Disintegration   57
Divergence   59
Deliverance   61

Part Three: Redemption   63

Dauntless   67
Destination   69
Dwelling   71
Depths   73
Dumbstruck   75
Divide   77
Desire   79
Drift   81
Dawn   83

ACKNOWLEDGMENTS

This book would not have come to life without the encouragement of my mother, Mimi, who fiercely believed that the world had to read my words and hear my stories.

I am ever so grateful for the privilege of having my own Muses in various stages of my evolution as an author: Genefel, Arlene, Valli, Simone and Mummie Taz.

SHIRLEY SIATON

INTRODUCTION

The poems in this book were all written during a particular era in my life when I could only successfully string words together if I had all these three things, without exception:

Coffee. *The stronger, the better. There was a point normal-sized coffee mugs could no longer cater to my needs.*

Music. *Preferably Noughties alternative and rock. I still write to the sounds of Evanescence.*

The Night. *In true tortured writer form, I could only write nocturnally. After midnight, to be exact.*

Thus, this collection came into being after one too many jaunts and musings in the dead of night.

I invite you to come dance with me, to the myriad rhythms of life, in these transcendental hours.

SHIRLEY SIATON

THE DANCE

Emergence

As with any dance and any journey, there is always a beginning, a starting point, an inception if you will.

This is a stage for looking at the world in wonder and, perhaps, later on, disgust and horror.

I have taken on the role of chronicler, more witness than partaker, as the stories unfold before my eyes.

Odyssey

It was time to move, to find my own place under the sun.

This is a treatise of a world I have lived in, one fraught with greed, destitution and despair. I have shared unfettered views of unforgiving cities and their dark corners.

Redemption

Each step was a tribulation, yet every path traversed was a triumph in the end.

The woman I am is a sum of all my tragedies and victories, hopes and dreams, loves and losses. There is sublime beauty in the dance of life, in the shadows and in the light.

SHIRLEY SIATON

Dance in the Dark

SHIRLEY SIATON

emergence

*All alone
in the silence
of endless thoughts
poured into an empty page*

SHIRLEY SIATON

DANCE IN THE DARK

SHIRLEY SIATON

Distance

All alone
In the silence
Of endless thoughts
Poured into an empty page.

The distance: a wall of
Isles, rocks and foam
Travelled on by despair;
Breaking through.

As blood pools
On the scrunched forehead-skin,
The soul had long since
Been lamenting

Chipped away
By time and blindness.
In the other world
It yearned to see.

SHIRLEY SIATON

Despair

Believe me
When I tell you that
I see hope in your eyes
Believe me
When I tell you that
I see strength in your pain
And my salvation in your
    carefully concealed despair

Believe me
When I look into your eyes
And say I see tears unshed
Believe me
When I try to touch your soul
But never could
And the cold simply
    rips my heart apart

Believe me
When I say goodbye
In a halting whisper
Believe me
When I turn away
From your compelling madness

Believe me
That I am sorry
    for being with you
That I love what I can
    never have
That I walk away from you
    before I no longer could

Believe me

Dark

I hope you will see
Right through the blankness
That is my countenance
It is not emptiness
But a mask of pain

I hope you will hear
Right through the quiet
That is my outward self
It is not silence
But a rage no one will understand
Hence I keep

SHIRLEY SIATON

I hope you will feel
The beating of my heart
That no one knows is still there
I am not stone
Nor darkness, nor torment
I am shadow
Wanting light
I am my unknown self
Needing you

Disruption

i. Lost

Brainfreeze
is all there is to it.
Nothingness
in my line of vision.

ii. Taken

You live in my head
Like cancer
You disrupt my system
As a virus would
A system embracing doom
In unguarded naiveté

You live in my head
Like a dream
You make me waken
In the dead of night
Breathless, empty, wanting
In the unforgiving dark

You live in my head
Like an echo
You speak without yielding
As the unwelcome does
An unwanted temptation
Taking me by storm

iii. *Sightings*

I am blind
I cannot see behind the mask
I pull over my own eyes
Like a curtain
My mask
My disguise

I am blind
I am bound
By my own darkness
My own unforgiving soul
My own expectations
My pride

I am blind
And I am safe
In this void
Where I remain
Untouched
Untouchable

Deception

Just don't listen to me
I lie
Time and time again
Until the falsehoods
Fall from my lips
As easily as breathing

Just don't say a word
I won't heed you
As always
You ask for nothing
You give everything
Without doubt

Just don't come any closer
I will push you away
With every moment
I am weaker
I am afraid
I can no longer hide

Just don't look at me
I can't bear the promise in your eyes
That you will fight for me
Without question
When asked to
But we are not just meant to be

Just walk away
Before I hold you back
Just leave
Before I run towards you
Just forget me
Before I learn to love you
Even more

Just stop

Discord

just like a razor
and its cutting edge
  voices and gazes of dissent
  slash through my flesh
but never draw blood

the cacophony of lies
from all around
  strike greater than a killing blow
  I painfully am close by
insurmountable I remain

the festival of unadulterated ugliness
and the breakdown it brings
  forces and persists against
  my indomitable will
unheeding I remain

SHIRLEY SIATON

Debt

Everything ends
As the sun upon the day sets
As throbbing lives crumble to ashes,
And dust
When turmoil eventually quiets

Everything is ephemeral
As facets of light glint upon the clouds
As moments become now,
And nevermore
Leaving only traces on minds and souls

Everything is not ours
When debts forgotten are collected
When our lives,
In borrowed time
Become defined by what we owe

SHIRLEY SIATON

Delusion

So steadfast and strong
This is how we believe
The powers and the promises to be
And so we become victims
Haplessly

So innocent and unhesitating
This is how we endure
The words and the creed written
And so we become pawns
Helplessly

So blind and ignorant
These we slowly turn out to be
As we fall into the trap of delusions
And so we become not the victor
Tragically

SHIRLEY SIATON

Danger

Displayed at each turn, beckoning
So easy to get, easier to possess
Every single morsel bearing
The promise of an easy buy
Irresistible

Spread out before our eyes, dazzling
So good to the touch, better to the pocket
Every single piece bearing
The marks of far-off places
Undeniable

Underneath the surface, lurking
So dangerous, what we cannot see
Every shred bearing the risk
    (of what it truly is)
The discarded and the unneeded
Expendable

SHIRLEY SIATON

Deprivation

There is emptiness
Resting inside my heart
Sitting, waiting, reverberating
With cries

There is emptiness
Thrumming in countless stomachs
Malevolent, ruthless, unrelenting
Eating away

There is emptiness
Shedding darkness on souls innumerable
Plotting, unkind, misdirecting
I yearn to cast aside

Divination

See there?

So many visions and dreams
Countless, now formless, pathless
Made and cast out in fearsome ritual
Since time immemorial

See there?

So many souls treading on the roads
Countless, now aimless, hopeless
With minds hungry for enlightenment
Only to be disillusioned

See there?

So much smoke streaming all around
Impenetrable, ever bringing greyness
If only the mist will rise
Give way to light
So we could once more see.

There.

Death

I know you—
a face among persevering faces
I have been told your story
countless times before
but salvation comes too late, each time

I heard you—
a voice among countless others
and the loud drumbeat
of a heart long since waiting
for Fate's kinder hand

Now
I wonder how it felt
for you to feel
the tearing of bullets
into your body and soul,
as the metal shrieked
and rent your dreams asunder.

SHIRLEY SIATON

odyssey

I toil against the storm
as it roars all around me
in a vengeful carnage
bringing death to dreams

SHIRLEY SIATON

DANCE IN THE DARK

SHIRLEY SIATON

Damnation

Every passing second
Is a hateful step closer
To an inescapable fate
Ever reminding
Of Time's irresistible power
Straight on to the very end

Every breath taken
Is made out of desperation
A final, futile bid for freedom
Ever hoping
That the air's purity would cleanse sins
Straight into immortality

Every drop of blood
Is hatefully alive
As it feeds the senses
Ever taunting
With lost chances and hopes
Straight into damnation

SHIRLEY SIATON

Dribble

I. Dribbling, dribbling
against the hardcourt
of your upper-lip stubble
in dark brown streaks
and streaky white.

II. Rivulets of hot fudge
sundae toppings
dispensed as
circular tracks or soot-stained snowflakes
into fragile plastic cups
taking the generous swell of
a beer belly.

III. Or my own
rounded stomach
(I so desperately try to conceal)
with the three-month life
you had spilled
into it.

IV. The way your choco fixes
lose themselves
to your voracious
appetite.
And greed.

Demolition

Spun all and sundry
In circles and whorls and loops
They took much
Out of nothing
That was already there.

There was hope
For tomorrow and warmth and bread
In the persevering form
Of desperately-constructed stalls
Rising from hot concrete.

Then heroes abound
In schemes and grandness and ambition
They bought desperation
With chunks of debris
Bringing an inevitable end.

SHIRLEY SIATON

Dreams

It is now time to see
Right through the turmoil
Running its course through our lives
And way beyond

It is now time to break free
Right through the ice
Locking us into a standstill
Forever buried beneath past sins

It is now time to wake up
Bring dreams to life and share a vision
Of our legacy unburdened and unchained
From transgressions past

SHIRLEY SIATON

Disease

A smile full of promise
A smile so glinting
The knife-edge of
Lying lips
A kiss for silver pieces.

A dance in the dark
A dance upon knives
The one-step, two-step is a
Rhythmic soundtrack
Into honor's doom.

A seduction unrelenting
A seduction so ruthless
The ticks are
Your beautifully dressed, coiffed
Death-bringers.

SHIRLEY SIATON

Defiance

I toil against the sun
As it beats down on me
In an evil haze of drought
Drying the sparse well of hope

I toil against the storm
As it roars all around me
In a vengeful carnage
Bringing death to dreams

I toil against desolation
As its hook cuts into my heart
In irresistible fatality
Denying the bounty of life

SHIRLEY SIATON

Duplication

Times two

It might be our only chance
To have what we have so longed for
It might be the only time
To get what we have asked for
But could never otherwise own

Times two

Will they ever heed our side?
They only care for their statutes
Those broken countless times before
For us, it would seem,
These remain ironclad

Times two

There is but irony
In this bitter play of fortune
To take what we need
Away from our hands
Away from our reach

Times two

Difference

As heaven against earth
There are no roads to take
Oceans to sail across,
or rivers to conquer
To bridge the widening gap

As heaven against earth
The land could be so far away
Beyond understanding,
this vicious circle
Of the rise and fall of hopes

As heaven against earth
The golden stairway to the sky
Is but an illusion
a broken promise of salvation
At the end of a rainbow unseen

Disintegration

Cracking away
This is one powerful fate:
The land has succumbed to
Without a shred of resistance

Falling apart
This is what we have turned into:
The pawns of power-driven dreams
Divided and moved as they will us

Vanishing into nothingness
This is the true danger:
That threatens our people
We begin to lose our very selves

SHIRLEY SIATON

Divergence

Here I am
At the crossroads
Of thought and memory and sensation
Awaiting the curtains to rise.

The ink
In the pen
Of unbridled spirit
Speak and question and speak
some more.

So unveiling
In brutal honesty
The halves and shadows along the way
That none may fall prey.

SHIRLEY SIATON

Deliverance

Away from the entrapment
Of their deceitful shrouds
And prettified lies
It was my time to live
This tribulation is my emergence

Away from being broken
By their enduring falsehoods
And stolen power
It was my time to rise
This tribulation is my odyssey

Away from being destroyed
By the hidden anarchy of old paths
And all-consuming greed
It was my time to strike
This tribulation is my redemption

SHIRLEY SIATON

redemption

*Make me see
all that I have to understand
so the raging inside
can quiet*

SHIRLEY SIATON

DANCE IN THE DARK

SHIRLEY SIATON

Dauntless

I stare into darkness
Wary, watching
Ever so calculating
And cold to the watchful eye

I speak to no one
With nothing to impart
But the blank slate that is my soul
That some say
Isn't there anymore
I hear nothing
Not their taunts
Or wishes for my supposed absolution
I am stone, strong, steadfast
Proud, invincible

I am unmoving
In the rain of time
In the thunder of pain
I am waiting for you
To let me feel again
Breathe again
Live again

SHIRLEY SIATON

Destination

Traverse the ocean
Let my voice swim
Through the rippling waves
Glittering
Beneath the golden sun

Traverse the sky
Let my heart soar
In the sheltering clouds
Embracing
My memories of home

Traverse the miles
That I may be there
Where I am most needed
Choosing
The road of tomorrow

Dwelling

Unyielding in your majesty
And proudly rising to the skies
You stand as silent witness
To conquest and pride

Incomparable in your mystique
And irresistible in your beauty
You are an honored paragon
Speaking of strength and freedom

Enduring in your virtue
And rich in your heart
You are the dwelling of dreams
Embodying hope
That could never be crushed

SHIRLEY SIATON

Depths

You have nothing, you say
Nothing to fight for
No reason to live or die
No battle, nor twisted reasons to lie
Just an empty heart beating
Deep into the moonless night

You have everything, you say
Everything to hate and shun
Pained endlessly
In the merciless light of the sun
All the countless whispers
Of judgment and persecution
Everything to carry, burdened evermore
Deep into your loneliness

You have me, you say
I to fight against, or madly hate
To die with, perhaps
To share your pain
In the harsh embrace of a cruel life
I gather the fragments
Of a heart long since unfound
And try so hard
To make you whole once more

And I have you, I say
To hold on to, to madly love
To live with—forever, perhaps
Or maybe beyond

In this unyielding existence
We shall find ourselves once more
So give me your heart
And we'll have our love to fight for

Dumbstruck

Now is not the time
To tell me that you're sorry
Just go on and don't look back
That's what I expect you to do

There is so much to say
Too many words rooted
In the depths of your eyes
You just can't put them to words

I've never said much, have I?
I'm mute as a mime when I'm near you
Then again, there's not much to say
For now, you're on your way

Don't say a word
Don't even look my way
Don't dare say you're sorry
Though I doubt I'll make it through
another day
Without you

SHIRLEY SIATON

I have not said I love you
And now I've lost the chance to
Say goodbye
Allow me one final embrace
That I will feel
Forever

Divide

I see the world
in a flood of dusty light-bulbs—
A vision pained by Time's merciless
inquest
Into a haggard soul;
But I plod onward.

Beneath a skylight
that threatens to cave in,
I bow my head in silent supplication
And my dreams scuttle away
Into the pages of a worn,
forgotten book.

I became a servant:
Hoping, waiting in vain
Until I am but a vegetable
Swimming in a lake of sweat and
depravity.

But the dust, too, shall tire and fall
And I will find the light
Streaming—first in puddles,
then in waves—
into my path.

Alone once more, I face
The beginning.
Alone once more, I know
There really is no end.

Desire

I feel my heart steaming towards you
I am wrought with the flames
    Of passion
        Consuming me
Until I am nothing more
        Than smoldering ash

I feel my body steaming towards you
I am drawn without resistance
        To your fiery seduction
        Burning deep into me
Until I am nothing more
        Than trembling desire

I feel my mind steaming towards you
I am controlled by this irresistible fascination
        And unrelenting obsession
        Taking over me
Until I am nothing more
        Than sheer madness

I feel my soul steaming towards you
I shall sweetly surrender
      All that I have
      And all that make me
Until I am nothing more
      Than your wasted possession

Drift

Make me see
All that I have to understand
So the raging inside can quiet.
In soothing tones
Hum a lullaby for me
Make the tears dry away
Into forgetfulness.

Seeking shelter–
Underneath its canopy
I could sing one last song of love;
Onward I will journey
Never to live
Back in the past.

SHIRLEY SIATON

Dawn

Eventide slowly falls
Under the stars
That blink and fool
Night becomes my shelter
In this cheerless solitude
Call to me
With your song
Ever promising

Dawn slowly rises
Over my wanting heart
Another waiting chance
For my redemption
Another life
Of nothing and everything
Time flows me by

Ever taunting
Present slowly comes
Enfolding and unfolding
Dawn and dusk
In a circle never-ending
Rising and falling
Eternally, so shall I go
Onwards and seeing

DANCE IN THE DARK

ABOUT THE AUTHOR

Shirley Siaton writes edgy and evocative poems and stories. Her worlds are in a deliciously dark cross-section of the romance, neo-noir, action, fantasy, new adult and contemporary genres.

She has several books of poetry and fiction released since February 2023. Her first book is the free verse collection *'Black Cat and other poems.'* She also pens juvenile literature as Shirley Parabia.

She is an award-winning writer, poet and journalist in English, Filipino and Hiligaynon, lauded by the Stevan Javellana Foundation, Philippine Information Agency and West Visayas State University. Her essays, short stories and poems have been published internationally in print and digital media. Her multi-lingual plays have been staged in the Philippines.

Shirley is a black belt in Shotokan Karate and an international certified fitness coach. Originally from Iloilo City, she is based in the Middle East with her husband and two daughters.

LINKS

Shirley's official website:
shirleysiaton.com

Complete reading guide:
shirley.pub

*Subscribe to Shirley's VIP list
for free exclusive updates:*
newsletter.shirleysiaton.com

www.ingramcontent.com/pod-product-compliance
Lightning Source LLC
LaVergne TN
LVHW040108080526
838202LV00045B/3827